CHRISTMAS UNSCRAMBLED

BOOKS FOR CURIOUS AND CLEVER KIDS

PAMELA PETTYFEATHER

PETTYFEATHER
PUBLISHING

CONTENTS

INTRODUCTION
WHAT IS CHRISTMAS?

Christmas is one of the most widely celebrated holidays in the world. But have you ever stopped to wonder where it all came from?

Why do we decorate trees and hang stockings? Who *really* was Santa Claus? What do reindeer, snowmen, and candy canes have to do with the birth of Jesus? And why do different countries celebrate Christmas in such totally different ways—from lantern festivals in the Philippines to barbecues on the beach in Australia?

In this book, we're going to unwrap the holiday season, piece by piece. You'll discover the ancient winter festivals that came before Christmas, meet the many gift-givers from around the world, and learn how traditions like caroling, Christmas cards, and festive feasts came to be.

But this book isn't just a history lesson—it's a holiday adventure!

Each chapter takes you to a different time and place, where you'll explore the fun, the faith, and the fascinating stories behind the world's most magical season. Along the way, you'll find puzzles to solve, recipes to try, games to play, and creative activities to help you make the season bright.

Whether you celebrate Christmas for religious reasons, family traditions, or just love the twinkly lights and treats, this book is for you.

So pour some cocoa, get cozy under a blanket, and let's dive into the snow-dusted story of Christmas—unscrambled at last.

🌲 Christmas Word Scramble

Can you unscramble these festive words? *(Psst... the answers are in the back of the book!)*

1. SLCUASNTAA

2. ERERDINE

3. EGHILS

4. EVESL

5. TOTMLSEEI

6. AIVTYNIT

7. GKTSNOCI

8. SRALCO

Let the holiday adventure begin! Turn the page and travel back in time to where it all started—with festivals of fire, feasting, and evergreen magic...

ANCIENT ROOTS: SATURNALIA, SOLSTICE & YULE

L ong before Christmas trees twinkled with lights or stockings hung by chimneys, people in the ancient world celebrated the darkest days of winter with joy, fire, and feasting.

That might sound surprising. After all, winter is cold, dark, and often gloomy. But for ancient civilizations, the winter solstice (the shortest day and longest night of the year) was a big deal. It marked a turning point: from this day forward, the light would begin to return.

So how did ancient people celebrate this magical moment? With some of the earliest—and wildest—winter festivals in history!

Saturnalia: The Roman Festival of Reversal

In ancient Rome, the most popular winter holiday was **Saturnalia**, held in mid-December to honor Saturn, the god of time and harvest. It was loud, silly, and full of surprises.

During Saturnalia:

- People exchanged gifts and lit candles.

- Masters served their slaves (yes, really).

- Everyone wore colorful clothes instead of their usual togas.

- Public feasts filled the streets.

- Gambling, singing, and jokes were everywhere.

The Roman God Saturn

It was a time to break the rules and celebrate life, light, and laughter. Sound familiar? Some of Saturnalia's traditions—like gift-giving and merry chaos—made their way into modern Christmas.

Winter Solstice: Welcoming Back the Sun

The **winter solstice**, which falls around December 21st in the Northern Hemisphere, is the shortest day of the year. Ancient peoples didn't have calendars like we do, but they watched the skies carefully. The solstice meant one powerful thing: the days would start getting longer. The sun was returning!

IN MANY CULTURES, this was a time for:

- Lighting fires and candles

- Holding festivals to honor the sun

- Feasting and storytelling during the long night

- Hoping for the return of warmth and crops in spring

Even today, some people celebrate the solstice with candlelight walks, music, and bonfires.

Yule: Norse Legends and Evergreens

In northern Europe, the Norse people celebrated **Yule**, a winter festival full of fire, feasting, and folklore. Yule is where we get some of the coziest and most magical Christmas traditions today.

The Norse God Odin

YULE TRADITIONS INCLUDED:

- Burning the **Yule log**, a huge piece of wood that was kept burning for days to bring good luck and light. (Today, it's often a chocolate cake shaped like a log!)

- Decorating with **evergreen branches**, which symbolized life even in winter's cold.

- Telling stories of the **Wild Hunt**, a ghostly procession across the winter sky led by Odin, the Norse god.

- Drinking **mead** and celebrating the return of the sun.

Yule celebrated the cycle of life, death, and rebirth—just like modern Christmas celebrates light returning to a dark world.

Fun Fact

The phrase "Yuletide" still pops up in Christmas songs like "Deck the Halls." It literally means "Yule time" and dates back over 1,000 years!

🌲 Create Your Own Winter Festival!

Imagine you live in a time before electricity, heat, or calendars. It's cold and dark... but the days are about to start getting longer. How would you celebrate?

USE these prompts to design your very own winter festival:

. . .

1. **Name of your festival:** _____

2. **Special food served:** _____

3. **What do people wear?** _____

4. **How do you celebrate the return of the sun?** (Music? Dancing? Bonfires? Giant cakes?)

WRITE a short description of your winter celebration. Bonus points if you give it a mascot—like a fire-breathing goat or a dancing snowball!

WITH ANCIENT FIRES blazing and evergreens in hand, winter holidays were already well underway... long before the first Christmas. But soon, a new story would change everything.

TURN the page to discover how the birth of a baby in a manger sparked one of the world's most enduring celebrations...

2

THE BIRTH OF CHRISTMAS:
THE NATIVITY STORY

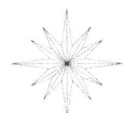

Now that we've explored the winter festivals that came *before* Christmas, it's time to discover how the holiday got its name—and what it's really about for billions of people around the world.

At the heart of Christmas is a story told for over 2,000 years: the **birth of Jesus Christ**. Whether you're religious or not, understanding the **Nativity story** helps explain why Christmas exists—and how it became one of the most important holidays in the world.

The Story Begins in Bethlehem

According to the Bible, over 2,000 years ago in the land of Judea (now part of Israel and Palestine), a woman named **Mary** and her husband **Joseph** were traveling to the town of **Bethlehem**. Mary was expecting a baby—but when they arrived, there was **no room at the inn!**

Instead, they stayed in a stable, where animals slept and straw covered the floor. That night, **Mary gave birth to Jesus** and laid him in a **manger** (a feeding trough for animals). This humble birth is known as the **Nativity**, which means "birth."

The Nativity Scene

Shepherds, Angels, and a Shining Star

According to the story, angels appeared in the sky to **shepherds** nearby, announcing the birth of Jesus and calling him a Savior. The sky filled with **light and song**, and the shepherds hurried to see the baby.

Far away, **wise men** (also called magi or kings) saw a **bright star** in the night sky and followed it to find the newborn child. They brought gifts of **gold, frankincense, and myrrh**—each with symbolic meaning.

The Nativity scene—Mary, Joseph, baby Jesus, animals, shepherds, angels, and wise men—is still one of the most iconic images of Christmas.

Why December 25?

The Bible doesn't say when Jesus was born. So why is Christmas celebrated on **December 25th**?

Most historians believe early Christians chose this date because it

aligned with Roman festivals like **Saturnalia** and the **winter solstice**, times already full of light, feasting, and celebration. The idea was to give people a new reason to rejoice—but keep some of the fun!

Christmas as a Christian Holiday

For Christians, Christmas is more than decorations or presents. It's a **holy day**—a time to remember the birth of Jesus, who they believe is the Son of God and a bringer of peace, hope, and love.

Churches around the world hold **midnight services**, retell the Nativity story, and sing **carols** (songs that share messages of joy and faith).

Even people who aren't religious often take part in these traditions because they're beautiful, peaceful, and full of meaning.

Fun Fact

In Spain and many Latin American countries, **January 6th**, not December 25th, is the biggest day for gifts and celebrations. It's called **Three Kings' Day** and honors the arrival of the wise men!

🌲 Nativity Quiz: Who's Who?

1. Who was the mother of Jesus?
   - A. Elizabeth
   - B. Mary
   - C. Martha

2. Where was Jesus born?
   - A. A palace
   - B. A stable
   - C. A temple

3. What guided the wise men to the baby?
   - A. A dream
   - B. A dove
   - C. A star

4. What gift was **not** brought by the wise men?
   - A. Gold
   - B. Silver
   - C. Myrrh

5. Who did the angels first appear to?
   - A. Shepherds
   - B. Soldiers
   - C. Rabbis

Answer Key on page 61.

Christmas began not with candy canes and Christmas trees, but with a newborn baby in a quiet town under a shining star. As the story spread, so did the celebration—and it kept growing.

NEXT UP: discover how carols, feasts, and fancy Christmas cards turned this holiday into a centuries-long tradition!

3

MEDIEVAL & VICTORIAN CHRISTMAS: FEASTS, CAROLS & CARDS

As Christianity spread across Europe, so did the celebration of Christmas. But it didn't always look the way it does today. In the Middle Ages and the Victorian era, Christmas evolved from a solemn religious holiday into a season of grand feasts, noisy games, and new traditions—some of which are still with us today.

Let's step into a time of knights, kings, candlelit banquets, and bustling Victorian streets to see how Christmas was celebrated centuries ago.

The 12 Days of Medieval Christmas

In medieval Europe, Christmas wasn't just one day. It was a twelve-day festival that started on December 25 and ended on January 6, known as Epiphany or Three Kings' Day. These twelve days were filled with food, music, dancing, and merrymaking—especially for those lucky enough not to work.

The holiday season was full of traditions:

- Houses were decorated with greenery like holly and ivy.

- Churches held elaborate services with Latin chants and candlelight.

- People sang carols—sometimes going door to door in exchange for food or drink, a tradition known as wassailing.

- There were grand feasts with roasted meats, pies, and fruit-studded puddings.

- A "Lord of Misrule" was often chosen to lead games, jokes, and mischief, turning the rules of everyday life upside down.

WHILE ORDINARY PEOPLE might have kept things simple, royal courts and wealthy families celebrated in style, with days-long banquets, plays, and masked dances.

The Lord of Misrule

The Pause and the Revival

By the 1600s, Christmas celebrations had become so rowdy that some religious groups, like the Puritans in England and New England, tried to ban them altogether. They believed Christmas should be a quiet, religious occasion, not a time for drinking and games.

But Christmas made a comeback in the 1800s—thanks in large part to one famous author: Charles Dickens.

Charles Dickens

The Victorian Christmas

When Charles Dickens published *A Christmas Carol* in 1843, he helped reimagine Christmas as a time of kindness, family, and generosity. His story of Ebenezer Scrooge, haunted by three spirits and transformed by the joy of the season, became an instant classic—and it still shapes how many people think about Christmas today.

Scrooge and the Ghost of Christmas Present, 1844

The Victorian era also gave us several modern Christmas traditions:

- **Christmas cards:** The very first printed Christmas card was created in England in 1843. Soon, people all over the country were sending colorful greetings by mail.

- **Decorated trees:** Queen Victoria's husband, Prince Albert (who was from Germany), popularized the tradition of decorating evergreen trees with candles, sweets, and ornaments.

- **Crackers:** Invented by a London confectioner, these paper tubes made a popping sound when pulled apart and contained small gifts or paper hats.

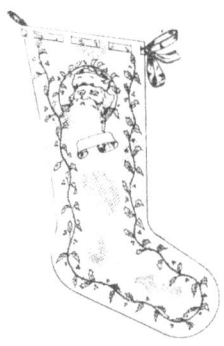

- **Gifts and stockings:** Small gifts placed in stockings hung by the fireplace became a cherished tradition for children.

Victorian Stocking

- **Caroling:** Victorian families revived old Christmas songs and added new ones, often singing them in the streets to raise money for charity.

Thanks to the Victorians, Christmas became more family-centered, sentimental, and joyful. It was also more commercial—stores began advertising holiday goods and encouraging people to buy presents, decorations, and cards.

Fun Fact

The phrase "Merry Christmas" became popular during the Victorian era—especially after Dickens used it in *A Christmas Carol*. Before that, people often said "Happy Christmas."

🌲 Design a Victorian Christmas Card

Grab a piece of paper and design your own Victorian-style Christmas card!

Your card should include:

- A festive border or frame

- An old-fashioned holiday greeting using fancy lettering. Make it rhyme!

- An old-fashioned illustration (a robin, holly, sleigh, or candle)

Vintage Christmas Card

🎄 **Carol Match Game:** *Match each famous lyric to its carol!*

LYRICS *(Hint: hum if you need to!)*

1. "All is calm, all is bright…"

2. "He sees you when you're sleeping…"

3. "O tidings of comfort and joy…"

4. "Let your heart be light…"

5. "Troll the ancient Yuletide carol…"

6. "Bring us some figgy pudding…"

7. "A partridge in a pear tree…"

CAROLS

A. Deck the Halls

B. Santa Claus Is Coming to Town

C. Silent Night

D. We Wish You a Merry Christmas

E. Have Yourself a Merry Little Christmas

F. God Rest Ye Merry, Gentlemen

G. The Twelve Days of Christmas

Answer Key on page 61.

If you don't know these classic carols, google them! They're great sing-a-long songs.

THE VICTORIANS DIDN'T INVENT Christmas—but they wrapped it in tinsel, added warm wishes, and delivered it with a card. As Christmas spread beyond Europe, different cultures added their own joyful touches.

NEXT UP: how one kind, gift-giving bishop turned into Santa Claus—and how the world celebrates him today.

SANTA CLAUS, ST. NICK
& THE GIFT-GIVERS

T oday, when most people think of Christmas, one jolly figure immediately comes to mind: Santa Claus. With his red suit, white beard, and flying reindeer, he's become one of the most recognized characters on the planet. But Santa didn't start out that way. His story is a patchwork of legends, saints, and storytellers from around the world—and he's far from the only holiday gift-bringer.

Let's travel through time and across continents to meet Santa's many cousins.

St. Nicholas: The Generous Bishop

The story begins with a real person: **Nicholas of Myra**, a Christian bishop who lived in what is now Turkey in the 3rd or 4th century. Known for his kindness and generosity, Nicholas was said to have secretly given money to help the poor—including a famous tale where he tossed bags of gold through a family's window (or chimney, in some versions) to save three sisters from hardship.

Over time, stories of his miracles spread, and Nicholas became a

Saint Nicholas of Myra

beloved saint—especially in Europe. December 6, the day of his death, became **St. Nicholas Day**, celebrated with small gifts and sweets for children.

In the Netherlands, St. Nicholas is known as **Sinterklaas**. He wears a bishop's robes, rides a white horse, and arrives by steamboat from Spain. Dutch settlers brought his legend to America, where his name slowly evolved into **Santa Claus**.

Santa Claus: From Poem to Pop Icon

The modern image of Santa began to take shape in the 1800s:

- In 1823, a poem titled **"A Visit from St. Nicholas"** (also known as *'Twas the Night Before Christmas*) described a plump, jolly man flying in a sleigh pulled by **eight reindeer**, delivering gifts by sliding down chimneys.

Thomas Nast's Santa (1881)

- In the late 1800s, political cartoonist **Thomas Nast** illustrated Santa for magazines, giving him a workshop at the North Pole and a list of who's been naughty or nice.

- In the 1930s, **Coca-Cola ads** helped solidify the red-suited, cheerful Santa we know today.

Though his look may be modern, Santa's message—generosity, joy, and kindness—is as old as the legend of St. Nicholas himself.

Santa's Global Cousins: Gift-Givers Around the World

Santa's not the only magical figure delivering gifts. Around the world, other characters fill his role—each with unique customs and stories.

La Befana

LA BEFANA (ITALY)

An old woman who rides a broomstick and delivers gifts on **January 6.** According to legend, she missed her chance to visit baby Jesus with the wise men and now travels each year leaving treats for children.

CHRISTKIND (GERMANY, Austria, Czech Republic)

A glowing angel-like child who brings gifts on Christmas Eve. Often pictured with golden curls and a halo, the Christkind is meant to represent the spirit of Christ. The name inspired the word **"Kris Kringle"** in America—another reminder of how holiday traditions travel and change around the world.

Julbock

THE YULE GOAT (SWEDEN & Finland)

In Scandinavia, one of the oldest Christmas symbols is the **Yule Goat**—called *Julbock* in Sweden and *Joulupukki* in Finland. The tradition comes from old Norse stories about the god Thor, whose chariot was pulled by goats.

Over time, the Yule Goat became part of Christmas celebrations, symbolizing strength and good luck. And people dressed up as the goat, knocking on doors and asking, "Are there any well-behaved children here?" (!)

In Sweden, the Yule Goat is now a straw decoration tied with red ribbons. In Finland, the *Joulupukki* has changed into a kind, Santa-like figure who brings gifts to children.

THE THREE KINGS (Spain and Latin America)

In Spain and Latin America, **January 6**—called **Three Kings' Day** or *El Día de los Reyes*—celebrates the Magi who brought gifts to baby Jesus.

On the night before, children leave out their **shoes**, often filled with **hay or carrots** for the kings' camels, hoping to receive small presents and sweets in return. In many cities, colorful **parades and street festivals** fill the evening, with people dressed as the Three Kings riding on floats and tossing candy to the crowds.

. . .

JULENISSE (NORWAY and Denmark)

A mischievous but kind gnome who wears a red cap and delivers gifts. He loves porridge, and families leave him a bowl on Christmas Eve.

DED MOROZ (RUSSIA)

"Grandfather Frost," a tall man in a blue or red robe who delivers gifts with the help of his granddaughter, Snegurochka. He visits on **New Year's Eve**, not Christmas.

Fun Fact

Reindeer aren't the only means of transport used by holiday gift-givers. In Switzerland, the Christkind sometimes rides a donkey. In Italy, La Befana flies on a broom.

🎁 FREE BONUS 🎁

Get global gift-givers' coloring pages (plus recipes from around the world & puzzles) in our *Christmas Unscrambled Bonus Pack*! **Scan the QR code below to get it!**

🌲 Match the Gift-Giver to the Country!

GIFT-GIVERS

1. La Befana

2. Christkind

3. Julenisse

4. Ded Moroz

5. The Three Kings

6. Joulupukki

COUNTRIES

A. Spain

B. Russia

C. Norway

D. Finland

E. Italy

F. Germany

Answer Key on page 61.

ACROSS CULTURES AND CENTURIES, gift-givers remind us of the same thing: the joy of giving, the wonder of winter, and the magic of a surprise.

AS WE TRAVEL into the next chapter, we'll explore how Christmas looks in different countries—sometimes snowy, sometimes sunny, but always full of cheer.

CHRISTMAS AROUND THE WORLD

C hristmas is one of the most widely celebrated holidays on the planet—but it doesn't look the same everywhere. While many people picture snow, reindeer, and evergreen trees, other countries celebrate with lanterns, fireworks, spicy food, or beach barbecues. Some celebrate in December, others in January. Some focus on Santa, others on the Three Kings, Christkind, or ancient traditions.

Let's take a sleigh ride around the globe to discover the dazzling variety of Christmas customs.

Mexico: Las Posadas and Piñatas

Piñata

In Mexico, Christmas is a long celebration that begins on December 16 and continues through January 6. One of the most beloved traditions is **Las Posadas**, a nine-night reenactment of Mary and Joseph's search for shelter. Each night, people go from house to house singing carols, holding candles, and ending with food, music, and **piñatas.**

Germany: Advent and Christmas Markets

In Germany, the holiday season begins with **Advent,** the four weeks leading up to Christmas. Many children count down the days using **Advent calendars,** which may have chocolate, pictures, or small toys behind each door.

A Weihnachtsmarkt stall

One of the most magical German traditions is the **Weihnachtsmarkt** (Christmas market). Town squares transform into winter wonderlands with twinkling lights, handmade ornaments, roasted chestnuts, and hot spiced cider called **Glühwein.** Wooden stalls sell gifts, and choirs sing carols under the stars.

Japan: A Holiday of Lights and Fried Chicken

Christmas is not a religious holiday in Japan, but it has become a popular celebration of love, lights, and fun. Cities light up with dazzling **illumination displays,** and couples treat Christmas Eve like Valentine's Day— sharing romantic dinners and giving gifts.

Surprisingly, the most popular Christmas meal in Japan is **fried chicken**—especially from KFC. Thanks to a clever advertising campaign in the 1970s, "Kentucky for Christmas" became a national tradition.

Instead of fruitcake or cookies, many families enjoy a **strawberry sponge cake** with whipped cream.

Philippines: The Longest Christmas in the World

In the Philippines, Christmas is celebrated from **September to January**—the longest holiday season on Earth. Decorations start going up as soon as the "-ber" months (September, October, etc.) begin.

One of the most beautiful traditions is the **Giant Lantern Festival** in the city of San Fernando. Local artists create enormous, glowing star-shaped lanterns called **parols**, which symbolize hope and light.

Families attend **Simbang Gabi**, a series of nine early morning Masses leading up to Christmas. Afterward, they enjoy treats like bibingka (rice cake) and puto bumbong (purple sticky rice).

Ethiopia: Ganna in January

In Ethiopia, most Christians follow the Orthodox calendar, which places Christmas—called **Ganna (also Gena)**—on **January 7**. The day begins with a dawn church service, and many people wear traditional white clothing called **shamma**.

After church, children often play a **game also called Ganna (also Gena)**, a fast-paced, hockey-like sport played with curved sticks and a wooden ball. The game is said to honor the shepherds who celebrated the birth of Jesus with joyful games and songs.

Instead of trees and stockings, the focus of Ganna is on **faith, family, and fasting**.

The Game of Ganna

Iceland: The 13 Yule Lads

In Iceland, children are visited by not one, but **13 Christmas trolls** called the **Yule Lads**. Beginning on December 12, a different Yule Lad arrives each night, leaving gifts in shoes placed on windowsills.

Each Lad has a unique name and personality—like Door-Slammer, Sausage-Swiper, and Spoon-Licker. If children misbehave, they might get a rotten potato instead of a treat.

Icelanders also celebrate **Jólabókaflóð**, the "Christmas Book Flood," where families exchange books and spend Christmas Eve reading by candlelight with hot chocolate.

Icelandic Yule Lad

Australia: Christmas in Summer

Since Christmas falls in the middle of summer in Australia, it's often celebrated with **beach picnics, outdoor concerts,** and barbecues. You're more likely to see people in swimsuits than sweaters, and Santa might arrive on a surfboard instead of a sleigh.

Carols by Candlelight events are held in parks across the country, where families gather under the stars to sing together. While some still

Surfboard Santa

decorate trees and hang stockings, the holiday has a sunny, relaxed vibe.

Fun Fact

The first country to officially declare Christmas a public holiday was **Armenia**, all the way back in the year 301.

🎄 **Match the Country to the Custom!** (*Answer Key on page 61.*)

COUNTRIES

1. Japan

2. Mexico

3. Germany

4. Philippines

5. Iceland

6. Ethiopia

7. Australia

CUSTOMS

A. 13 trolls deliver gifts in shoes

B. Tamales and piñatas during *Las Posadas*

C. Lanterns and early-morning Masses

D. KFC dinners and strawberry shortcake

E. Barbecues and beach celebrations

F. Midnight church service and spicy stew

G. Christmas markets and Advent calendars

. . .

CHRISTMAS MAY HAVE STARTED as a small celebration in one part of the world—but today, it's a global holiday filled with color, creativity, and community. No matter the language, weather, or traditions, one theme shines through: joy shared across generations.

NEXT UP: discover the meaning behind the most iconic Christmas colors, plants, and decorations.

SYMBOLS OF THE SEASON

C hristmas is one of the most visually rich holidays in the world. From evergreen trees to twinkling lights, from holly berries to shiny stars, the season is full of meaningful symbols—many of which come from ancient traditions long before Christmas existed.

But what do they all mean? Why do we decorate with red and green? What's the story behind mistletoe, and why do we top the tree with a star or an angel?

Let's explore the hidden meanings behind the most iconic Christmas symbols.

The Evergreen Tree: Life That Lasts

The tradition of decorating **evergreen trees** started in northern Europe. For ancient peoples, the evergreen tree—one that stayed green even in the coldest, darkest days of winter—was a symbol of **hope, strength, and life that endures.**

In the 1500s, Germans began bringing small trees indoors and decorating them with candles, fruit, and later, paper ornaments. The tradition spread across Europe and eventually to America, where the trees became brighter, taller, and more elaborate.

Today, the Christmas tree is one of the most beloved decorations of the season—whether it's real or artificial, simple or full of sparkle.

Red and Green: The Colors of Christmas

The colors **red** and **green** dominate everything during the holiday season—from wrapping paper and sweaters to ribbons and wreaths. But their connection to Christmas goes back centuries.

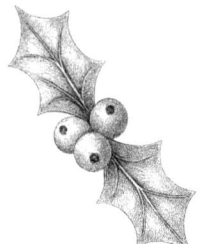

- **Green** symbolizes **life, nature, and renewal.** In winter, when most trees are bare, evergreens remind us that life continues even in dark times.

Holly Berries

- **Red** is the color of **holly berries,** which were used in ancient winter festivals. In Christian tradition, red also represents **the love and sacrifice of Jesus.**

Together, red and green create a bold, festive contrast that brings warmth to winter.

The Star: A Light in the Darkness

Many families place a **star** at the top of their Christmas tree. This represents the **Star of Bethlehem,** which—according to the Nativity story—guided the wise men to the place where Jesus was born.

The star has come to symbolize **guidance, hope, and wonder**—a light shining through the darkness.

Some families use an **angel** instead of a star, representing the angels who announced Jesus's birth to the shepherds.

Wreaths and Holly: Circles of Life

Christmas Wreath

A **wreath** is a circle made from evergreen branches, sometimes decorated with red berries, ribbons, or pinecones. The circle shape has no beginning or end, which makes it a symbol of **eternity and the cycle of the seasons.**

Holly, with its spiky green leaves and bright red berries, has been part of winter celebrations since ancient times. Romans used holly to honor Saturn during Saturnalia. Later, Christians saw the red berries as a reminder of Christ's sacrifice, and the sharp leaves as a symbol of the crown of thorns.

Mistletoe

Mistletoe is one of the strangest holiday plants. It grows high in trees, has no roots in the ground, and stays green year-round. Ancient Druids considered it sacred and believed it had healing powers. In Norse mythology, mistletoe was a symbol of peace.

Over time, mistletoe became a symbol of **love and goodwill.** The tradition of kissing

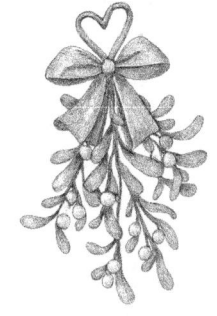

Mistletoe

under the mistletoe began in Victorian England, where it was believed that anyone caught standing beneath it had to accept a kiss.

While kissing is optional, the mistletoe's message is clear: peace, affection, and connection.

Lights and Candles: Chasing Away the Dark

In ancient times, people lit fires and candles during the winter solstice to keep away darkness and evil spirits. As electricity spread, candles were replaced with **twinkling lights** on trees, windows, and rooftops.

Today, Christmas lights create a sense of **wonder and warmth**, reminding us that even during the darkest days of winter, there is still light to be found.

Bells, Candy Canes, and Stockings: More Meaning Than You Think

- **Bells** were originally used to **announce good news** or call people to church. Today, they also symbolize **celebration and joy**.

- **Candy canes** may have started as simple shepherd's crooks given to children during church services. The

red and white stripes are said to represent purity and
sacrifice.

- **Stockings** are hung by the fireplace in honor of the St.
  Nicholas story, where he dropped gold into stockings hung
  to dry. The tradition continues, filled with surprises and
  treats.

Fun Fact

The tallest Christmas tree ever displayed was in Seattle in 1950. It
stood 221 feet tall—taller than a 20-story building.

🌲 Create Your Own Holiday Symbol

What new holiday symbol would you want to invent? Use the ques-
tions below to brainstorm.

- What does your symbol represent? (Peace? Friendship?
  Imagination?)

- What shape is it?

- What colors would it use and why?

- Where would people place or display it?

- What traditions or meanings would grow around it?

🎄 **Match the Symbol to Its Meaning!** (*Answer Key on page 61.*)

SYMBOLS

1. Evergreen Tree

2. Star

3. Wreath

4. Holly

5. Mistletoe

6. Lights & Candles

7. Candy Cane

8. Stockings

9. Bells

MEANINGS

A. Crown of thorns and Christ's sacrifice

B. Light shining in darkness

C. Peace, love, and goodwill

D. Shepherd's crook and purity

E. Eternity and the cycle of seasons

F. Life that lasts through dark times

G. St. Nicholas's secret gifts

H. Guidance, hope, and wonder

I. Joy, celebration, and good news

FROM STARS and trees to mistletoe and firelight, Christmas symbols help us celebrate more than a single day. They connect us to the past, to each other, and to the stories we pass on.

NEXT UP: explore the festive flavors and international feasts that bring people together.

CHRISTMAS FEASTS & TREATS

W hat would Christmas be without something delicious to eat? Across the world, food is at the heart of Christmas celebrations. Whether it's a slow-cooked stew shared after church, a slice of fruitcake with tea, or a steaming cup of cocoa by the fire, every culture has special meals and treats that mark the season. And like many Christmas traditions, the foods we eat have stories behind them.

Let's take a seat at the world's holiday table and discover how families everywhere celebrate Christmas through food.

Roasts, Puddings, and Mince Pies: A British Christmas Feast

In England and other parts of the UK, Christmas dinner is a big deal. The centerpiece is often a **roast turkey or goose,** served with gravy, potatoes, stuffing, and vegetables. Many families also enjoy **Yorkshire pudding,** a puffy, eggy bread roll served with the meal.

For dessert, there's **Christmas pudding**—a dense, spiced cake made with dried fruit, nuts, and sometimes a splash of brandy. It's

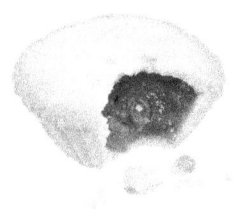

Mince Pie

traditionally made weeks in advance and steamed on the stovetop. Some people even light it on fire before serving.

Then there are **mince pies**—small pastries filled with a sweet, spiced fruit mixture. Hundreds of years ago, they actually contained meat. Today, they're a sugary holiday favorite.

Panettone and Pandoro: Italy's Christmas Cakes

In Italy, Christmas sweets are works of art. The most famous is **panettone**, a tall, fluffy bread-like cake filled with raisins and candied orange peel. It's often served sliced with butter or cream.

Panettone

In northern Italy, families may prefer **pandoro**, a golden, star-shaped cake dusted with powdered sugar. Its name means "golden bread," and it's just as festive as it sounds.

On Christmas Eve, Italian families may enjoy a **Feast of the Seven Fishes**, a seafood-based meal served in many Italian-American homes. It's a way to honor tradition, family, and the anticipation of Christmas Day.

Tamales, Turrón, and Tropical Fruit: Christmas in Latin America

In Mexico and Central America, **tamales** are a must. These steamed corn dough pockets are filled with meat, cheese, or beans, wrapped in corn husks or banana leaves, and often made in giant batches by the whole family.

Tamales

In Spain and Latin American countries like Colombia and Peru, people enjoy **turrón,** a chewy nougat made with honey and almonds. Fruit, hot chocolate, and rich rice dishes also fill the table.

On Christmas Eve, called **Nochebuena,** families gather for a late-night feast filled with music, fireworks, and food passed down through generations.

Gingerbread and Lebkuchen: Germany's Spiced Delights

Gingerbread House

Germany gave the world **gingerbread houses,** inspired by the fairy tale of Hansel and Gretel. But long before that, Germans made **Lebkuchen**—spiced cookies sweetened with honey and flavored with cloves, cinnamon, and nutmeg.

At Christmas markets, vendors sell Lebkuchen hearts decorated with icing and hung on ribbons. Children bake and decorate gingerbread cookies in the shapes of stars, angels, and animals.

Nigeria: Jollof Rice, Goat Meat and Dodo (Fried Plantains)

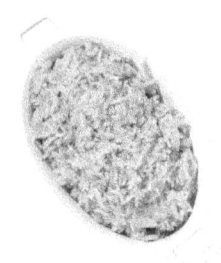

Jollof Rice

In Nigeria, Christmas is a time for vibrant celebration and community. Streets fill with music, church choirs sing in every language, and families travel long distances to gather at home.

The centerpiece of the feast is **jollof rice** —a colorful, spicy dish made with tomatoes, peppers, and onions—served with **chicken, dodo (fried plantains)**, and **goat meat.** Everyone helps cook, and the meal is shared with neighbors and guests, often followed by dancing late into the night.

Christmas in Nigeria blends faith and festivity—a joyful reminder that good food tastes even better when shared.

Julbord: Sweden's Christmas Buffet

In Sweden, the holiday meal is called **Julbord,** meaning "Yule table." It's a buffet-style spread with pickled herring, gravlax (cured salmon), meatballs, ham, and boiled potatoes. For dessert, there's **risgrynsgröt**, a creamy rice pudding often served with cinnamon.

Risgrynsgröt

A fun tradition: a whole almond is hidden in the rice pudding. Whoever finds it is said to receive good luck—or be the next to marry.

The Philippines: Noche Buena and Sweet Treats

Lechon

In the Philippines, Christmas is one of the longest and happiest celebrations in the world—beginning in September and lasting past the New Year! After midnight Mass on Christmas Eve, families gather for **Noche Buena**, a joyful feast filled with laughter, gifts, and song.

The table overflows with dishes like **lechon** (roast pig), **pancit** noodles, **hamón**, and **queso de bola** (round cheese). For dessert, there are sweet rice cakes such as **bibingka** and **puto bumbong**, often sold outside churches by candlelight. Christmas in the Philippines is about family, food, and togetherness—celebrated with warmth and music that fills the tropical night.

Christmas Cookies: An American Tradition

In the United States, Christmas cookies are everywhere. Families bake batches of sugar cookies, gingerbread men, peanut butter blossoms, and peppermint bark.

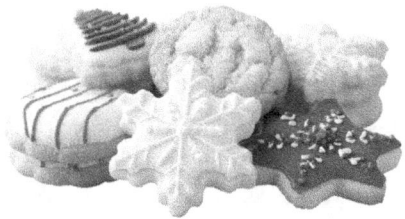

Christmas Cookies

Many people leave a plate of cookies and a glass of milk out for Santa Claus on Christmas Eve. Others host cookie swaps or decorate cookies with icing, sprinkles, and andy.

The custom likely started with European immigrants who brought baking traditions with them and added American flair.

Other Festive Foods Around the World

Bûche de Noël

- **France:** Bûche de Noël (Yule log cake), oysters, and foie gras

- **Greece:** Melomakarona (honey-dipped cookies) and baklava

- **Poland:** Wigilia meal with 12 meatless dishes on Christmas Eve

- **Ethiopia:** Doro wat (spicy chicken stew) with injera flatbread

- **Australia:** Prawns, barbecued meats, and pavlova (a meringue dessert)

Fun Fact

The tradition of making gingerbread men is said to have started in the court of Queen Elizabeth I, who had cookies made in the likeness of visiting dignitaries.

🎄 Design Your Dream Christmas Menu

What would your perfect Christmas meal look like? Fill in your answers below.

- Main dish: _____

- Side dish: _____

- Dessert: _____

- Special drink: _____

- What would your meal be served on (or with)? (Fancy plates? Picnic blankets? Snow?)

🌲 Christmas Feasts & Treats Quiz

1. What is the traditional centerpiece of a British Christmas dinner?
    A. Roast turkey or goose
    B. Ham and pineapple
    C. Roast beef

2. What's special about Christmas pudding?
    A. It's steamed and made weeks in advance
    B. It's frozen
    C. It's eaten cold for breakfast

3. In Italy, what is *panettone*?
    A. A tall, fruit-filled cake
    B. A sweet rice pudding
    C. A bread made of chocolate

4. What is the main ingredient in tamales, a Latin American Christmas favorite?
    A. Rice
    B. Corn dough
    C. Potatoes

5. What is *turrón* made from?
    A. Honey and almonds
    B. Chocolate and mint
    C. Coconut and sugar

6. Germany is famous for which spiced holiday cookie?

    A. Biscotti

    B. Lebkuchen

    C. Macarons

7. In Sweden, what is the Christmas buffet called?

    A. Fika

    B. Smörgåsbord

    C. Julbord

8. In the United States, what treat is often left out for Santa Claus?

    A. Cookies and milk

    B. Cocoa and marshmallows

    C. Candy canes and tea

9. In Ethiopia, the traditional Christmas dish *doro wat* is a kind of

_____.

    A. Bread

    B. Chicken stew

    C. Rice pudding

10. What do Australians often eat for dessert on Christmas Day?

    A. Pavlova

    B. Fruitcake

    C. Gingerbread

Answer Key on page 61!

ACROSS COUNTRIES AND CENTURIES, food has been a way to celebrate love, tradition, and togetherness. Whether sweet or savory, familiar or new, a Christmas meal is about more than just what's on the plate—it's about who's gathered around it.

UP NEXT: discover how Christmas continues to evolve, and how people are reimagining the holiday.

Hungry? Want to taste the some of these global Christmas flavors?

Scan the QR code to download the **FREE Christmas Unscrambled Bonus Pack!**

Try simple recipes from around the globe—plus puzzles and games to keep your brain cooking!

CHRISTMAS TODAY: FUN, FAMILY, AND GIVING

Christmas started long ago with ancient festivals and sacred stories—but it's far from stuck in the past. Every year, families around the world keep rewriting it with their own sparkle and style. Some hold tight to old traditions; others invent brand-new ones. Either way, the spirit stays the same: joy, togetherness, and giving.

A Holiday for Everyone

More than 160 countries celebrate Christmas. In some, it's a holy day remembering the birth of Jesus. In others, it's a season of lights, laughter, and community cheer.

In sunny places like Australia or Brazil, people grill on the beach and dance under the stars. In snowy towns, families sip cocoa, light candles, and swap stories by the fire. Even those who don't celebrate religiously often join in the kindness and generosity the season inspires.

Old Traditions with New Twists

The classics still shine—but they've learned new tricks.

- Trees can be real, reusable, or even digital.

- Carols mix with pop beats.

- Paper cards turn into animated e-cards.

- Kids video-chat with Santa or track his sleigh online.

Christmas keeps evolving—one remix, meme, and emoji at a time.

Tech Makes It Together

Families separated by oceans can still open presents "side-by-side" on video calls. Social media turns cookie-decorating into global show-and-tell. Apps organize Secret Santa swaps or digital Advent calendars. Even Santa's gone high-tech—you can text him, call him, or design your own virtual ornament.

Greener and Kinder Christmases

Today's celebrations aren't just merry—they're mindful.

- LED lights save energy.

- Fabric gift bags replace single-use wrap.

- Homemade gifts and local shopping cut waste.

- Families donate old toys before unwrapping new ones.

The goal: spread joy *and* take care of the planet we share.

The Gift of Giving

Beyond ribbons and boxes, Christmas giving means generosity. Around the world, people volunteer, donate food, or help neighbors in need. Schools and communities host coat drives, toy swaps, and kindness challenges. The best gifts, kids soon learn, can't be wrapped —they're shared.

Fun Fact

Every year, NORAD (the North American Aerospace Defense Command) tracks Santa's flight path live online on Christmas Eve. Millions of kids---and adults!---visit the site to see where he is in the world.

🌲 **Your Christmas, Your Way**

No two Christmases look alike—and that's the magic. Maybe yours means pajama-movie night, caroling, or cookie contests. Maybe it's reading a favorite story or writing a "gratitude letter" each year. Traditions grow with families, and every one tells a story.

So—what story will *your* Christmas tell? Reflect on your own ideal Christmas celebration.

MY FAVORITE PART of Christmas is:

ONE TRADITION I love (or want to start) is:

IF I COULD CREATE a brand-new holiday tradition, it would be:

A GIFT I'd like to give someone that doesn't cost money:

ONE WAY I can help someone this season:

Help Santa find his sleigh!

CHRISTMAS ISN'T JUST about what has been---it's about what we make it. It's a holiday that grows with us, shaped by the things we value most: family, love, creativity, and care for others.

Now that we've explored Christmas past and present, are you it's time to have some (more) fun!

Download the **FREE Christmas Unscrambled Activity Pack** for extra puzzles, games, and global recipes! Test what you've learned and keep the Christmas spirit going.

Scan the QR code below!

ANSWER KEY

Introduction: Christmas Word Scramble

1. **SLCUASNTAA** → SANTA CLAUS

2. **ERERDINE** → REINDEER

3. **EGHILS** → SLEIGH

4. **EVESL** → ELVES

5. **TOTMLSEEI** → MISTLETOE

6. **AIVTYNIT** → NATIVITY

7. **GKTSNOCI** → STOCKING

8. **SRALCO** → CAROLS

Chapter 2: Nativity Quiz

1. B. Mary.
2. B. A stable.
3. C. A star.
4. B. Silver.
5. A. Shepherds.

Chapter 3: Caroling Match Game

1. C. Silent Night
2. B. Santa Claus Is Coming to Town
3. F. God Rest Ye Merry, Gentlemen
4. E. Have Yourself a Merry Little Christmas
5. A. Deck the Halls
6. D. We Wish You a Merry Christmas
7. G. The Twelve Days of Christmas

Chapter 4: Match the Gift-Giver to the Country

1. E. Italy
2. F. Germany
3. C. Norway
4. B. Russia
5. A. Spain
6. D. Finland

Chapter 5: Match the Country to the Custom

1. D. KFC dinners and strawberry shortcake
2. B. Tamales and piñatas during *Las Posadas*
3. G. Christmas markets and Advent calendars
4. C. Lanterns and early-morning Masses

5. A. 13 trolls deliver gifts in shoes
6. F. Midnight church service and spicy stew
7. E. Barbecues and beach celebrations

Chapter 6: Match the Symbol to Its Meaning

1. F. Evergreen Tree – Life that lasts through dark times
2. H. Star = Guidance, hope, and wonder
3. E. Wreath = Eternity and the cycle of seasons
4. A. Holly = Crown of thorns and Christ's sacrifice
5. C. Mistletoe = Peace, love, and goodwill
6. B. Lights & Candles = Light shining in darkness
7. D. Candy Cane = Shepherd's crook and purity
8. G. Stockings = St. Nicholas's secret gifts
9. I. Bells = Joy, celebration, and good news

Chapter 7: Christmas Feasts & Treats Quiz

1. A. Roast turkey or goose
2. A. It's steamed and made weeks in advance
3. A. A tall, fruit-filled cake
4. B. Corn dough
5. A. Honey and almonds
6. B. Lebkuchen
7. C. Julbord
8. A. Cookies and milk
9. B. Chicken stew
10. A. Pavlova

MORE BOOKS FOR
CURIOUS & CLEVER KIDS

GLOBAL EXPLORATIONS. HISTORICAL EXCAVATIONS. FUN ACTIVITIES.

Welcome to the Books for Curious & Clever Kids series—a collection of lively nonfiction books that bring world traditions, history, and cultures to life for kids ages 7–12!

UNSCRAMBLED HOLIDAYS

The *Unscrambled* series explores the real history and global traditions behind the holidays we celebrate today. Each book traces where a holiday began, how it changed over time, and how people around the world mark it now, blending clear explanations, surprising facts, cultural context, and fun activities and puzzles. Designed for curious middle-grade readers, the series helps kids see familiar holidays in a whole new way—beyond the cards, candy, and decorations.

Unscramble Valentine's Day, Saint Patrick's Day (2026) Easter, May Day, Independence Day (2026) Halloween, Thanksgiving (2026) and Christmas!

EDUCATIONAL COLORING BOOKS
EXPLORE CULTURE THROUGH COLORING

Books that pair short articles, activities and coloring pages for kids ages 8-12 to make learning more fun and coloring more enriching! Available in paperback and durable hardcover.

Fraudulent Folklore: A Cryptid Coloring, Fun Facts & Creative Writing Book

Color your way through the world's most famous myths, monsters, and misunderstood legends—then discover what's fact, fiction, and wildly exaggerated. History, folklore, and a healthy dose of skepticism.

The Gilded Age Coloring Book: America's Age of Splendor

Step into an era of opulence, ambition, and scandal, where tycoons built empires and society glittered on the surface. This coloring book brings the drama, style, and contradictions of the Gilded Age to life.

All the Kings & Queens of England Coloring Book

From Alfred to Elizabeth II, meet every king and queen who shaped

England's turbulent history. Coloring book-style famous portraits and short bios make this a lively tour through centuries of rule.

Meet the Presidents of the USA:
A Presidential Coloring Book

Meet every U.S. president, from powdered wigs to modern politics, through engaging portraits and approachable historical snapshots. Perfect for curious minds who want history to feel human—and fun.

New Year's Customs Around the World:
A Global Traditions Coloring Book

Ring in the New Year with customs from around the globe, from fireworks and feasts to lucky foods and ancient rituals. A joyful, international celebration of how cultures mark fresh starts and hopeful beginnings.

All books available on Amazon.

BONUS CHRISTMAS ACTIVITY PACK!

Scan the QR code to download your **Bonus Activity Pack**—a festive thank-you from us to you!

Get **UNSCRAMBLED** with **_EXTRA_** puzzles to test what you've learned—plus simple, kid-friendly recipes for Christmas treats from around the world. **Learn, play, and celebrate the joy of the season... one puzzle and cookie at a time!**